Cecil Bødker

MARY of Nazareth

Pictures by Bengt Arne Runnerström

Translated by Eric Bibb

R&S
BOOKS

Stockholm   New York   London   Adelaide

The sun was already high over the mountains; it was midmorning. Ann had lingered at the well to chat with the other women. Now she had to hurry home. Her feet moved quickly under her wide skirt, stirring up the yellow dust with every step she took.

It didn't take long for Ann to reach the narrow alley where she lived. Once inside her own yard, she lifted the large, heavy water jug from her head and placed it in the shade.

She stopped to listen; it was so quiet. Had Mary, her daughter, already finished grinding the flour for baking?

Ann went over to the storehouse and pushed open the door. There sat Mary on a sack of grain with her hands clenched, staring straight ahead with wide-open eyes.

"Mary, what's wrong? Are you not feeling well?" asked Ann.

"I'm going to have a baby," whispered Mary. "That's what the man who was here told me."

"Who? What man?"

"It was a stranger," Mary mumbled. "I've never seen him before. He just appeared. Suddenly he was standing right in front of me."

Ann saw that Mary was trembling and put her arm protectively around her. "Did he hurt you?"

"I don't know. I was so afraid. He said I would give birth to a child, and that I shouldn't be sad, because it would be a holy child. What do you think he meant by that?" Mary began to cry.

Ann laid a hand on her forehead, which was burning. "You're sick," she said. "You must have been dreaming."

Mary shook her head.

"Well, now try to rest," said Ann and spread a blanket over Mary.

Ann went out into the yard and began preparing the evening meal. When Joachim returned from his work in the fields, everything seemed to be back to normal.

"Where's Mary?" he asked.

"She's sleeping," said Ann as calmly as she could. "She has a fever." And then Ann told Joachim everything that Mary had said.

"I've never heard of anyone getting pregnant from a common fever," said Joachim, snorting.

Mary, who was listening to their conversation, didn't dare move. It was clear that her father was very upset. What would Joseph, her fiancé, say?

"I must speak with Joseph," said Joachim. He went out, slamming the gate behind him.

Ignoring the midday heat, Joachim made his way through the narrow streets to Jacob the carpenter's house. Jacob himself answered the door.

"I want a word with your son Joseph," said Joachim brusquely.

Joseph appeared and looked questioningly at his future father-in-law, but Joachim didn't say a word. He walked away from the house and anyone who could hear them, and Joseph followed in silence. Joachim didn't stop until they reached the outskirts of the village, where the vineyards began.

"Is it something about Mary?" Joseph asked cautiously.

"She says she's with child," said Joachim. The words were like a blow to Joseph.

"Do you think that I'm responsible?"

"I don't think that it's you. I would see it on your face if it were, but I had to make sure," said Joachim.

"God help him if I meet him," said Joseph. But he sounded uncertain, and his face had turned very pale.

"I don't want to talk about it," said Joachim.

Joseph remained silent. Then he turned abruptly and headed back to the village.

Ann was aware that everything had become very different since the other day. She lifted the water jug onto her head and went to the well as usual, but even from a distance she felt the other women watching her. What had they been talking about before she arrived?

"I hear your Mary is sick," said one woman.

"No one has seen her for several days," said another.

"Mary has a fever," said Ann shortly.

"Oh, is that why Joseph has stopped visiting her?" a third voice added.

"Maybe that's why he had an argument with Joachim," said the woman who had spoken first.

"An argument. What makes you say that?" Ann felt the anger burn inside her. All she wanted was to get to the well and fill her jug. The women were sure to discuss the little she had said and add it to their own explanations. Perhaps they already suspected that Mary was pregnant before she was supposed to be.

At noon, Joachim came home to eat.

"They're talking," said Ann. Joachim understood immediately that she meant the other women in the village.

"Already?" he muttered. I'm really not surprised, he thought. Mary had always been well behaved, kind, and obedient. It hadn't been difficult to find a suitable husband for her.

"I've been thinking," Ann said. Then she paused. "Maybe we should send her away from home for a while," she said finally.

Joachim looked at his wife in astonishment. "And where do you think we should send her?" he asked.

"She could stay with Elizabeth and Zacharias. It would probably be a good thing for Joseph as well if she went away."

"Mary has never traveled alone before," said Joachim in a low voice.

"Elizabeth and Zacharias aren't strangers to her," said Ann. "They're our relatives."

"Very well, then," said Joachim, sighing. "But don't tell her until after I've left."

When Joachim had gone, Ann cautiously explained to her daughter that perhaps it would be wise for her to go and stay with Elizabeth for a while. Mary looked at her mother with surprise.

"But she's going to have a baby, too," said Mary. "He said that my Aunt Elizabeth was in her sixth month and she would give birth to a son." Ann stared at Mary. As long as they had been married, Elizabeth and Zacharias had wished for a child, without having one. And suddenly Mary claimed that Elizabeth was pregnant now when she was clearly too old for such a thing.

"I'm not making it up," said Mary. But it sounded strange even to her own ears, so she didn't dare continue.

When Joachim came home that evening, he told them that he'd talked to a merchant's servant. He'd made arrangements for Mary to travel with the merchant's caravan the day after tomorrow, two hours before sunrise.

"There's no need to worry," said Mary to Ann when the two of them were alone. "It is as if I've been meant to visit Elizabeth all along."

The more Mary thought about her coming journey, the less it worried her. If it really was true that she would give birth to a child whose birth had been determined in the days of the Prophets, then nothing could harm her or the child.

They rose in the middle of the night in order to be on time. The sky was still dark when Joachim helped Mary up onto the donkey. She couldn't take much with her: a sleeping mat, gifts for Elizabeth and Zacharias, a little bread and dried dates for the journey, and a goatskin bag with water.

Mary felt as if she were being watched, even though no one could be seen. It was a relief to come out onto the path that led up to the highway where the caravan was waiting. When they were still quite a distance away, she recognized the smell of camels. Soon she could also make out the sounds of the people who were loading them for the long trek.

Mary knew she would be traveling with the caravan for three days before they reached Jerusalem. The last bit of the journey to Ein Kerem, where her relatives lived, would surely take no more than another day if the merchant managed to find someone who was going that way.

By afternoon, the caravan had arrived at a little village surrounded by shady trees. The camel drivers let the camels drink, and then Mary gave her donkey water and tethered it under a tree. After taking a drink herself, she filled the goatskin water bag, which she had emptied during the morning. She sat down with her bread near two other women.

"Are you traveling alone?" asked one of the women when they finished eating.

"Yes," said Mary.

"You're not traveling far, are you?"

"To my relatives in Judea," said Mary. "My Aunt Elizabeth is expecting a baby," she added quietly. The women looked closely at her body when they thought she wasn't looking.

"And when is the baby due?" they asked. Mary smiled to herself. She knew what they were thinking.

"She's in her sixth month," she said. They didn't ask any more questions, but both of them eyed her suspiciously. It was unusual to see a young woman traveling alone, and it was clear that they had their own ideas about the reason — the real reason.

After the midday stop, the caravan continued its journey until the light disappeared from the sky. They reached the inn where they would pass the night. The camel drivers slept out in the open with their camels. They lit a campfire and wrapped themselves in their sleeping mats.

The caravan reached Jerusalem around noon on the third day. The only times Mary had been there were during the Passover holidays, and she would never have been able to imagine the way it usually looked. People worked in open shops that faced the streets. All sorts of buying and selling were going on. Men drove donkeys before them, laden with goods, and yelled for people to make way for them in the narrow streets. Women balanced baskets and jars filled with wares on their heads.

Immediately after they arrived, the caravan leader began asking around and succeeded in making arrangements with a merchant who was traveling west into the mountains. Mary had to describe where she was going as specifically as possible so that a price could be settled upon.

"Are you going to see the priest Zacharias?" asked the clothing merchant. "Wasn't he the one who had a revelation? They say he hasn't uttered a word since."

Mary shuddered. A revelation?

Early the following morning, she set out with her new companions. When they stopped to eat and drink, Mary asked the clothing merchant what kind of vision Zacharias had had.

"They say it happened in the Temple when he was offering incense in the Inner Sanctum. It was before the altar. Outside, people were praying. When the priest finally appeared, they could tell immediately that something was wrong. 'What has happened?' the people shouted. Zacharias tried to speak, but he couldn't make a sound."

The closer they came to the village of Ein Kerem, the more convinced Mary became that there was a connection between what had happened to her and the events in the Temple. Now she was also certain that she would be received well by her relatives.

But when they arrived in the afternoon and Mary knocked on the gate, she found it locked. She had to knock many times before it was opened by a servant with a broom in his hand.

"The priest is not at home," said the man.

"That doesn't matter," said Mary quickly. "I'm here to visit his wife, Elizabeth."

"She hasn't received any visitors for more than five months."

"But surely she will accept a gift," said Mary, taking a folded length of cloth from her traveling bundle. It was a soft, finely woven cloth, the kind women often used to swaddle their newborn babies.

"Take this to her and say that it is from Ann and Joachim's daughter, Mary of Nazareth." When the man finally returned, he seemed upset and looked at Mary suspiciously, almost as if afraid of her.

"Elizabeth began to cry when I gave her the cloth," he said.

"I'm sure they were tears of happiness," said Mary. "I'll go in and speak with her."

Elizabeth was still crying when she came toward Mary with outstretched arms.

"Mary," she said. "It's really you. But how in the world did you know? The child, the child, it moved inside me for the first time. Just when I realized what kind of cloth it was and heard your name, he kicked. I'm so happy." Elizabeth put her arms around Mary.

"I'm carrying a new life, too," said Mary softly.

"I know. I knew it as soon as I saw you. Zacharias has told me that a child will come after mine. He has had a revelation and he says that which was prophesied long ago is about to be fulfilled."

"But I thought Zacharias couldn't talk," Mary said in astonishment. "Isn't he still mute?"

"He moves his lips," Elizabeth said. "In that way I can read the words. He told me that it was Gabriel who appeared before him and said that I would give birth to a son." Gabriel, thought Mary. The Angel Gabriel, was he the one who had appeared before her?

"It feels as if you were destined to stay with us," said Elizabeth.

Later, Zacharias returned home. He was very pleased when he saw Mary from Nazareth and he welcomed her graciously. Zacharias and Elizabeth had a little room prepared for Mary right away.

When Mary had been with her relatives for three months, Elizabeth gave birth to a son. Mary rejoiced with the happy parents, but inside she longed for her home. However, she promised to stay until the circumcision celebration was over.

On the day of this important event, the whole house was bustling with activity from very early in the morning. Zacharias personally went around to make sure that everything was as it should be. The special priest who would perform the circumcision had arrived the evening before. Two strong servants built a huge fire that would burn down to glowing embers over which an ox would be roasted. Mary was overwhelmed by it all.

The circumcision itself, which took place on the eighth day after the boy's birth, was performed inside the house in the presence of the adult male relatives and as many neighbors as space allowed. But when it came to the actual name-giving, none of the witnesses knew what the boy would be called.

"Of course he shall be called Zacharias after his father," someone said.

"His name will be John," said Elizabeth. She glanced at her husband, who nodded for her to continue. "It has been said that he will have that name even though it is not in our family," Elizabeth announced.

Everyone turned to Zacharias. He made the sign of a square in the air, and Elizabeth summoned a servant to bring a writing tablet. Zacharias took it and wrote with a stick in the soft wax. Then he held up the tablet for all to see, and those who were able to read aloud for all the others: "John."

"Of course he shall be called John when we say so," said Zacharias suddenly. The room fell completely silent. "That was my voice!" he exclaimed in amazement. "I'm talking! I'm talking!" he shouted so that he could be heard all the way out in the yard.

And with his arms raised over those assembled, he burst into song, giving thanks for the newborn child and the return of the gift of speech.

Those present agreed that the boy John would become something special, when such things could occur. Rumors spread quickly about the strange events at the priest's house during the circumcision celebration.

Shortly thereafter, Mary returned to her parents in Nazareth.

Once home in Nazareth, Mary worried that Joseph would forsake her. She was sad, because she had become very attached to him during their engagement.

One day, Mary's father came home after visiting the house of Jacob the carpenter, and told them that Joseph had decided it was best that they break their engagement. He and his brothers and his father felt it was the right thing to do.

Mary bowed her head and pressed her hands together when she heard this. Now was the time to be strong. This was the price she must pay for being chosen, but it was almost unbearable. What would become of her?

But one evening, a few days later, Joseph himself paid a visit to Joachim's house. He wanted to tell of a dream he had had.

Joachim showed Joseph to a bench against the wall of the house. Ann and Mary also came over to listen to what Joseph had to say.

"I had a dream," said Joseph, taking his time. "I dreamed that what I intended to do was wrong. I no longer wish to end my engagement to Mary. I want to marry her, even though she's expecting."

Joseph's words burned like fire within Mary. She cried quiet tears of joy for being reunited with Joseph. Now she would have a normal life. She wouldn't have to live alone as an outcast or be forced to support herself as a prostitute.

The only thing left to do was to explain it all to Joseph's own family. In the eyes of his father and brothers, he had no right to bring a child of unknown origin into the family. By going against the accepted customs, he would be offending his people. And yet he felt that it was the right thing to do.

Joseph got up, and before leaving, he asked for permission to visit Mary as he had done before.

A decree had come from the Romans, saying that everyone must travel to the town of their forefathers to register for taxation. The families of Mary and Joseph were of the house and lineage of David and therefore had to make their way to Bethlehem.

As quickly as they could, they made the necessary arrangements and set out. Many others were traveling the same road — it was almost as if the whole world was in upheaval.

Once again, Mary sat on her father's donkey. This time she was dressed in an ankle-length cloak that Joseph had given her.

"It's a shepherd's robe," Joseph had said. "It will protect you from both rain and wind."

When at last they came to Bethlehem, it was late in the afternoon. The city was full of travelers and all the inns were already full.

Mary said nothing. Now and then she felt a sharp pain, and she knew she was about to give birth. Ann noticed and decided that she would personally ask for lodgings at the next inn. Finally she was shown to a place in a little stable which had been carved right into the mountain. There, in one of the stalls, a fresh bed of hay had been placed on the ground so that the innkeeper and his wife would have somewhere to sleep when all the other places were taken. Reluctantly, they offered the place to Ann. Joachim and Joseph lifted Mary down from the donkey and carried her into the stable.

In her traveling bundle Ann had packed everything needed at a birth. At times she had dreaded that Mary was carrying a demon inside her, and it was a great relief for her when late that night Mary gave birth to a healthy boy-child with arms, legs, fingers, toes, and a face like all other normal babies.

The following day Ann went with Joachim to register, and after one more night in the stable they returned home. But Joseph and Mary remained with the baby in Bethlehem. Mary was still too tired to get up, so they had to wait a while before going to register for taxation.

In the afternoon of the day that Mary's parents had left for home, there was suddenly a commotion at the back door of the inn.

"Some shepherds have come," said Joseph to Mary, who was lying in the hay, feeding the baby.

"We have seen a sign!" called one of the shepherds to the innkeeper. "A great light in the sky above your house. What has happened?"

"Nothing at all has happened here," shouted the innkeeper, "except that she" — and the innkeeper pointed to his wife — "has let some young woman give birth to her child in the only place left for me to sleep."

This meant that the baby had been born under the bright light.

"May we see the child?" one of the shepherds asked timidly.

They crowded in front of the doorway and looked in at Mary, who protectively drew the baby closer to her.

"What child is this?" they asked. "Perhaps the boy will be someone great who will come to mean much to us all."

"Yes," Mary said softly. She wished the boy were an ordinary child. Somehow, it felt as if the prophecy might take him away from her.

Mary longed to be home in Nazareth.

When the boy was barely a week old, Joseph came and told Mary about some foreigners that he'd seen out in the street.

"Some men from a distant land, dressed in fine clothes. I heard them asking the way to the inn. They said they followed a sign in the heavens and that they had spoken with some shepherds in the fields north of the city."

Then the innkeeper himself appeared and opened the door to the stable. This time he reverently stepped aside for the distinguished guests.

Mary was frightened and drew even closer to the wall, cradling the baby in her arms.

"You have nothing to fear," said one of the strangers. "We have come to greet the newborn. We want to honor him and offer our gifts."

"We are stargazers, and we come from Babylon, in Mesopotamia. A great leader of the Jews of Israel has come to the world in the person of this child."

"We have seen his sign three times in the sky, most recently in Jerusalem. Everything is as the Prophets of old have predicted."

The men commanded their slaves to bring forth the chests that they had brought with them on their journey. They opened them on the floor of the stable and took out gifts made of the purest gold. The strangers bowed and sang, and they left all the valuable gifts when they departed.

For a long time Mary sat with the baby on her lap and thought about the remarkable events of the past week.

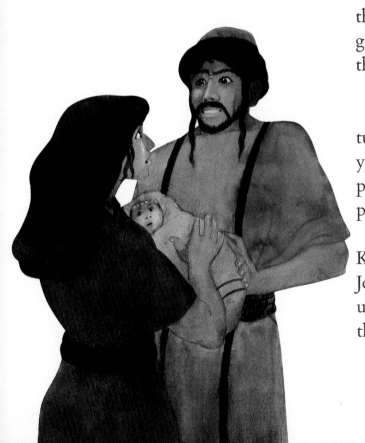

The time was now approaching when, forty days after the birth, the boy must be presented at the Temple in Jerusalem. Mary and Joseph had discussed turning over the gifts to the Temple because they were afraid of having to keep such treasures themselves. When it was time, Joseph hired yet another donkey and wrapped the chests in rags so they wouldn't attract too much attention.

On arriving in Jerusalem, they went directly to the Temple to store the chests somewhere safe. The priest who received them was very surprised to see this simple couple leading a donkey laden with objects made of the purest gold. Joseph and Mary explained that they were gifts for the boy. The priest then called a meeting with some other priests to decide what should be done.

"It must be the child," said one priest. "The one that King Herod seeks."

After a quick conference one of the priests said: "We have been ordered to turn this child over to the king if we find him. But don't be afraid. Carry out your errand at the Temple, present the boy, leave your offering, and then go in peace. Do not speak a word to anyone of what kind of child this is. Move to a place where no one knows you. Leave this land for a time."

On the way back, Joseph and Mary thought about what the priest had said. King Herod knew that the Prophets had predicted that a true leader for the Jewish people would be born in Bethlehem at the appointed time. They understood that Herod would kill the child if he found him, because he would threaten Herod's power as king.

Joseph and Mary set out and kept to the poorest areas on the outskirts of the city. Carefully Joseph headed their donkeys in a southernly direction, but Mary noticed anyway.

"Quiet," Joseph whispered to her. "Wait until we're beyond the city, and I'll explain. We're going to take the great caravan route which leads to the south."

"Out into the desert?" asked Mary in dismay. "I thought we were on our way home to Nazareth!"

"I've had another dream," said Joseph. "We will travel to Egypt. No one must know where we are."

"Isn't it very far to Egypt?" asked Mary cautiously after they had ridden for quite a distance in silence.

"Yes, it is," said Joseph. "But we will be safe there. King Herod has no power in Egypt."

That evening they reached the caravan site in Hebron. Joseph managed to buy places for them by selling both their donkeys.

After several days' journey across the desert, they passed over the border into Egypt. Mary felt discouraged. Everything was so strange to her here, and she didn't understand one word of the language being spoken around her. Joseph didn't understand Egyptian either, but in the beginning he was assisted by a camel driver who interpreted for him. Soon he had learned enough to get by on his own.

"I know where the Jews live in this city," said Joseph to Mary.

The Egyptian Jews in Heliopolis received them warmly and helped them with everything as they were getting settled. They were able to rent a house that had long been vacant, and they moved in with their boy.

In time, Mary grew accustomed to the way people lived in what was one of Egypt's largest cities. Everything which in the beginning had been strange and foreign became part of her everyday life.

Joseph had found work as a shipbuilder's apprentice. Mary also enjoyed working with her hands. Wearing a long robe, she could carry her little boy while she shopped at the market or weeded their small vegetable patch which lay outside the city.

Now and then Joseph went to the caravan sites to ask the camel drivers for the latest news from their homeland. The most recently arrived caravan had such terrible news that Joseph almost didn't dare tell Mary. The Roman soldiers had been looking for their boy in Bethlehem. King Herod thought the boy was being hidden there. When the soldiers couldn't find him, the king became furious. To be rid of this one child, he ordered the soldiers to kill all boys under the age of two throughout the city.

Mary grew pale when Joseph told her this. Are we to blame, she wondered, for all those boys dying just so our child might live?

One day, Mary asked Joseph if he, too, longed to see his village, his family, and his father's workshop.

"Of course," said Joseph. "But when we return I want to have my own workshop. I've learned many new skills here that I would like to make use of at home. I couldn't do so if I still had to work for my father."

One day, news of King Herod's death reached Mary and Joseph. Now it would finally be possible to return home.

They had been in Egypt for three years. Their house had gradually been filling up with beautiful things, and now they sold most of them to pay for their journey aboard a ship which would carry them across the sea to Palestine.

As they came closer to home, Mary and Joseph thought of all the familiar things they would see again after being away so long. What had happened in their village while they were gone?

Mary's parents, Joachim and Ann, were overjoyed to see them again. They had been sure that they had seen the last of their daughter.

Mary's boy was now three years old. Ann thought he looked like any other child. His name was Jesus.

Ann saw that the childish qualities in Mary had completely disappeared. She was now a serious young woman. Mary and Joseph were determined to have a home of their own, and it wasn't long before Joseph began building it.

As soon as the house was ready, they moved in and began living like everyone else in the village. Joseph did well with his work and Mary looked after their home. Before the year was over, Mary gave birth to her second child. Just as she'd imagined, it was good for the oldest son to have a new family member to help care for. And in the eyes of their neighbors they became just another family.

Mary and Joseph eventually had more children — both sons and daughters.

Since Joseph had attended the synagogue school when he was a boy, he naturally wanted his own sons to be educated there. He wanted them to know the history of the Jewish people as it had been written down in ancient times and as it had been told from one generation to the next.

When the children were old enough, Joseph and Mary brought them to Jerusalem to take part in the Passover festivities. There they would celebrate the High Holidays together in the Temple. They also got to know their relatives from other parts of the country.

Mary was very happy to see Elizabeth from Judea. With her she could speak freely about her oldest child's future. Mary was concerned about Jesus. He sometimes asked her questions that were impossible to answer.

The year that Jesus turned twelve, he was allowed to accompany Joseph into the men's outer courtyard at the Temple during Passover. This was a sign that he was approaching manhood.

On the way home from Jerusalem, Joseph and Mary lost track of Jesus, but they didn't worry too much. The older children were permitted to travel with other families that had children the same age. It took a while for them to begin wondering whom Jesus was actually traveling with.

"We're sure to see him when we rest for the night," said Joseph.

But that evening they couldn't find him either, and Joseph and Mary decided to turn back the following day to look for him in Jerusalem.

They were now quite worried. Where could their boy be? For two whole days and nights they looked for him, hardly sleeping at all.

On the third day Mary and Joseph gave up their search and went to the Temple to pray and find comfort. It seemed so deserted everywhere now that the crowds and all the music and singing were gone. There was only one square still alive with activity. Priests and learned men sat and stood around in a tight circle, with their backs to those who passed by.

"What's going on over there?" asked Joseph in a whisper.

"It's that boy," someone said. "He's asking questions. He was here yesterday, too."

Joseph stood on tiptoe to get a better look. He was able to see a boy sitting cross-legged in the middle of a circle of bearded, serious-looking men.

"Why, it's Jesus!" exclaimed Joseph, and called Mary.

"That's my boy!" said Mary, loudly and clearly.

It became completely still. All conversation stopped. The boy looked up and caught sight of his mother. He seemed to be looking at Mary from somewhere far away.

"Where have you been all this time?" she asked.

"Here," he answered in a surprised voice. "I'm twelve years old now. I'm allowed to be here."

"We thought something had happened to you."

"Why did you come looking for me?" he asked. "Don't you know that this is my father's house? But now I'll come home with you," he said calmly. And he followed them out of the Temple.

Mary didn't scold Jesus anymore. She was very happy and relieved to find him unharmed and healthy. But both she and Joseph thought about the events of the past days. On the last day of their journey home, Joseph told the boy that it was time for him to start helping out at the workshop.

"If you want, I can make a good craftsman out of you," he said. "I'll teach you everything that I have learned."

"Yes, Father," said Jesus.

And the morning after their return to Nazareth, Jesus followed Joseph into his workshop to begin learning his father's trade. In time, Jesus would probably become a fine carpenter, thought Joseph.